PRAISE FOR *CLOCK STAR ROSE SPINE*

"Wilde charts worlds of light and liquid that slide through space-time, myth and imagination awash with the mundane."

—Laura Gray Street, author of *Pigment and Fume*, coeditor of *The Ecopoetry Anthology*

"Fran Wilde is one of my favorite contemporary writers. These poems are powerful, elegant, precise maps and directions and destinations that make me long to travel again—at least to the places inside Fran's imagination, from Hades to Los Angeles. A gorgeous collection."

—Theodora Goss, author of *The Strange Case of the Alchemist's Daughter*

"Fran Wilde's poetry makes my heart soar, and then ache, and then soar again. The lyricism of her prose has been quietly upping the stakes for language in speculative fiction for years now, and we're so fortunate to get such a potent, concentrated dose of it here."

—Sam J. Miller, author of *The Blade Between*

"These poems turn on truly colorful ideas—what if you married the sea and had known each other since elementary school—kudos Fran Wilde. It's a book to go back to."

—Samuel R. Delany, author of *Dhalgren*

Clock
Star
Rose
Spine

FRAN WILDE

LANTERNFISH PRESS

CLOCK STAR ROSE SPINE

Lanternfish Press
399 Market Street, Suite 360
Philadelphia, PA 19106

lanternfishpress.com

Cover Design: Kimberly Glyder
Text Design: Megan Jones Design

Printed in the United States of America.

Library of Congress Control Number: 2020952690

Print ISBN: 978-1-941360-57-6

Digital ISBN: 978-1-941360-58-3

CONTENTS

TO ALL THOSE WHO
COLOR OUTSIDE THE LINES

I

Clock:

COMPASS ROSE

CLOCK STAR ROSE SPINE

This could be a poem in quatrains
—North, South, East, West—
four dividers pointing different directions
towards a completed whole.

In the first quatrain, a stilled compass,
limbs spread, spine spun
to star-crossed cardinal points, sunlit.
(You are at work while I write this.)

Horizon ahead, the distances behind me
and you are traveling.
This quatrain defines the middle points
—West of South, Northwest, Southeast, East of North—

this could be a sestina, if I had two more points.
Lines form a rose, a clock, a star, a spine.
East: I once woke on a dock, splintered wood against my back when
the sun rose.
You weren't there.
North: I slept on a train station floor, cold marble beneath my head,
a star.
You were beside me.
West: I woke at a strange hour, strange light, and me a stopped
clock,
positive I'd dreamed myself to another country—
we don't talk about it.

South: The moment light crosses your face. My anchor. My spine—
you smile awake beside me.
I'm dreaming this now.

This could be an aubade.
One with an empty pillow, a sense of many ways to turn.
I thought I'd write a poem about the marks
life leaves on skin. The drag of distance

against knowledge, experience—
your eyes on mine, that compass
that now, the where and the way it tethers me.

A star, a rose, a clock,
points of possibility
spun on a central spine.

THE FACT OF A CAGE

A trapped sky, no matter
how vast, how pretty—

how safe.

A series of gates—
too small to pass through.

INSTRUCTIONS FOR HOW TO FEEL

Must be spare and strong
Must not take up room
May not shout it
May not get things damp
Shouldn't cause too much discomfort
Should not break things
Just the right amount of wit
A few pauses where
Someone else can put their own
Another can say of course this
Or that
Was what she meant
Must not disagree
Must not scream and bite and scratch
Must be the right feeling
For the moment
Don't fight it

SELF PORTRAIT WHILE BEARING
THE WEIGHT OF OTHERS

That kick in the middle
Just below the sternum

That sense everything is noise, anticipation
And nothing is sense, or release

A group of friends gathers
Like geese to nibble at cake

at how big you are getting
and to lace you in ribbons

while you worry that your mother
feels left out because she will

that kick in the middle
reminds you how to span many lives

often supported
        sometimes stretched translucently thin.

YOU ARE TWO POINT THREE METERS
FROM YOUR DESTINATION

Commencing Route for Orpheus of Thrace.

Proceed from Ciconian Coast meadow south-southwest to mouth of
Eurotas River in Laconia, approximately eight hundred kilometers.
Travel time to waypoint: seven days at your current speed.

✻

Head ninety-two kilometers south to Cape Taenarus, also known as
Matapan. Find Taenarus Gate.
Recalculating. Find Taenarus Gate. Proceed to route.

✻

Pass into Taenarus Gate and proceed to River Styx.
A toll is required. Exact change is required.

✻

Proceed to route. Descend five thousand kilometers to throne room.
Time to destination: unknown.

✻

Arriving at throne room. Proceed five point two meters to throne.
Avoid abyss. Make your request.
Receiving new information from satellites. Calculating return trip.

✻

Exit throne room, follow northern path to Vale of Avernus, Cicero, Italy. Approximately six thousand kilometers.

Proceed up incline. No turns are permitted on this route.

○

Proceed up incline. You are five hundred meters from your destination.

No turns are permitted on this route. You are one hundred meters from your destination.

You are two point three meters from your destination. Proceed up . . . recalculating.

○

Recalculating. Proceed to route.

Proceed to . . . No crossing of the River Styx is possible at this time.

○

Proceed to route. Recalculating. Proceed ahead from River Styx, approximately five thousand kilometers to the mouth of the Acheron River.

○

Calculating new destination. Proceed six hundred kilometers north-northeast through forest to Rhodope Mountains. Time to destination, five days to three years. Several drinking establishments ahead on left.

○

New route selected.

IF/THEN

I would strip myself to the metal
      and start again.
I would rewire everything
      to more standard settings
      better code.
The market demands stronger, less
      of some things, more of others
I would go out one door
And come in another
      so different. So extraordinary.

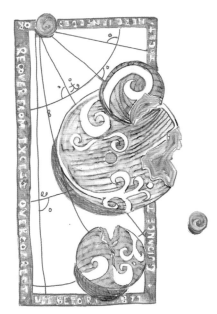

MAPS

At year's end
　　we erased the maps,
　removed rivers,
　　　　deleted borders.

We cut
　　the compass out,
　　　　　tried to navigate
　　by the gap remaining.

Where will you go?
　　Departing friends
　　　　worry
　　　　　we have nothing to guide us.

But as the year begins
　　　we take the map's pieces
　　　　and reassemble
　　　　　road and compass
　　　　　river and gap
　　　to make our own direction
　　　to keep moving
　to change with each step
　　so we cannot be lost.

A RESUME

Goals include: meaningful work, using my skillset,
>   preferably by the sea.
Experienced in shipwrecks, sea chanteys, hospitality.
Career highlights: You've heard of Odysseus? A rare near miss.
>   Also search party experience,
>   though Demeter wasn't thrilled with the outcome.
Close call at a singing competition, but Hera rigged that.
>   Orpheus too.
Languages spoken: Greek and Latin.
References: Achelos at RiverGods, Inc., several Muses,
>   and my equally talented sisters.
Willing to relocate.

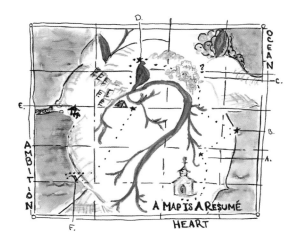

SELF PORTRAIT AS A DISTANCE

A sweep of light cuts sea
from storm, cuts
hull from reach of rocks.
A lighthouse knows night, at least;
is sure what's hull, what's sea, what's storm.
The lighthouse is firmly anchored, unlike

this weak boat it protects and judges.
But when shore's left behind
when light sinks below horizon,
when instruments swing on their bearings,
a quartering sea rises and falls,
hard as rock, shaking my hull until only one star shines straight

then disappears; the broken clouds pull closed
and memory goes dark for now
I float I float I float

Star:

A LIE IS A FLAT SURFACE

BREAKFAST POOLSIDE AT THE LAFAYETTE

San Diego

A turquoise pit of light
framed in cement, striped hotel awnings,
white slat chairs, taupe loungers, where

a 1940s era audience slouches, ghosts, all knowing
azure is a seductive color
        unintended. It lures the eye.

I rest in shadows, out of the bright.
My glass rests on a napkin: rippling rings of blue across white.

At far-flung tables, breakfast arrives.

Coffee. Eggs, easy. Crisp bacon.
"You aren't starving. Slow down," one man says;
"It's delicious." His partner places a forkful of omelet between his
teeth.
"How can it be delicious? It's hotel food."
"Maybe because I want it to be."

Another couple sips tea, silently reading news
        from glowing screens—small pools drowned in sunlight.

Near the deep end, a shadowed plaque declares

Tarzan designed this pool.
        (Tarzan was designed by one
        Johnny Weissmuller,

        the iconic call,

the broad swimmer's chest.)
I wish to put my ear to the sign's brass shell,
        its historic surfaces,
eavesdrop on Larry Imig, the Lafayette's owner

calling Weissmuller about the pool.
        His list of Hollywood wants:
        a space to lure the stars out in sunlight;

a terrazzo suitable for Ava Gardner's feet;
        300,000 gallons of turquoise shaped by a leading man:

regulation-Olympic, a volume of water
        enough to hold Bob Hope's laugh, to let it echo
        across time, to me,
        here in the shadows, surrounded by ghosts.

In 1940, when they poured the terrazzo,
        they mislaid a board.
All of Tarzan's measurements skewed,
        but no one noticed.
I wonder how many starlets were passed around like poolside
drinks, tall and cool.

I wonder if Johnny Weissmuller ever in the middle of the dark San
Diego night
    was tempted to a Tarzan yell—
        and if everyone laughed, entertained.
The past flickers in shadows, black and white:
struggling to last against bright morning light and the smell of
bacon.
Hollywood's ghosts: Names on plaques, a mislaid board
that makes the pool shorter than it claims to be.

I'm waiting out the worst of the sun with the ghosts,
waiting until I can re-enter the world as myself, swim the water.
The sun crests the pool deck, casting light in new directions

and I must shift my chair.
The woman breakfasting nearest me
chews so loudly I can hear the bacon break from where I sit.
    She devours the news, sizing up each starlet,
their indiscretions, for her husband.
"Look at her, she's had work done.
    That kind of thing leaves a mark, forever."

The light is too bright and I tire of fearing it.
On the back of a now-damp napkin, I make a list

 of reasons it's not safe to go out in the sun,

not safe to be known, a star in daylight.
My list is six months of travel, of glare and smiling,
    and finding the shadows when I could.

Judgments flow onto paper in turquoise ink.
I hold myself to one per month so I don't shout from the brightness
and ruin breakfast, so nice by the pool.

On airplanes, in hotels, strangers grabbing me from behind.
In a cab, a driver asking about my family,
　　　telling me he can get my phone number off the database.
Overheard, a fan saying, "She smiled at me, I can do what I want."
In black tie, a business partner, leaning, "You sure clean up nicely."
I cross them all out.

There's too much sun, too much of everything and I am

too sensitive.

Ghosts of poolside starlets hiss like wind
　　and scatter my notes.
The woman rolls her eyes.
　　　"You won't believe *this* one."
I stay alone, in the shadows,

by a pool just short of official length.
A mislaid board. A quirk.
That kind of thing leaves a mark on a terrazzo.

Cutlery rings against white china.
Chairs screech backwards on tile.
Brunch is over, the air-caught napkins
　　hit the water and sink,
the ink bleeding tendrils of blue through the bright.

LOOKING BACK: EXHIBITION IN RED

A museum is a book we travel.
Brush past pale walls, thought-speckled,

push into retrospective:
through broad, hemic
watercolor, crimson gouache
past bodies
bent backwards, giving breath, birth.
Past silent shouts and revolutions
to a quieter chapter.

The lithographs take us this time
the way each familiar letter deep pressed
to the page carves

ascender and descender
driving ink against paper and mark
the careful geometry
of a city lived in and reflected on
a grid of pulp

the opposing wall, sanguine
dye shapes breast and organ,
moment and message. Each
regular edge, each soft form
centers itself in strict windows.
Each a bright letter

to the city, the book, the museum
that says
we are pieces and the sum
of our pieces,
containers and contained,

always rebelling
against restrictions
of wall and page,
blooded and bloodied.

After Louise Bourgeois Retrospective, MoMA 2017–18

SELF PORTRAIT WITH FRIDA KAHLO

alongside *Fulang-Chang and I (1937; assembled after 1939)*

If you, with this mirror, frame me,
affix me on a wall to look over you,
to witness your pain; to weigh knife glint and scar
like a doctor, would you also, pretty Thoth, see mine?

Does a body earn its place beside you, in your life's work,
stilled, while the mirror's face shifts and, to be honest, is too short
to show more than eyes and a hairline, a few small scars;
my cane is out of view, my braces hide under fabric and time,

and I'm so good at concealing everything, while you
rend yourself with paint, frame yourself
with hard edges? I would slip from this gallery like water,
until there is only silvered glass trapped in a rigid frame.

Time ties you immortal to canvas and paint.
I exit the mirror, a whisper, a feint.

A CATALOG OF LOST NEGATIVES

We drive from Cleveland to Pine Ridge in four days.
Cross the national parks, sleep in our car,
photograph red hills, bone-dry; bars and trees;
one moose. A lot of dogs. Some sunrises.
We find a hostel hidden deep in Wyoming
after our car breaks down, liquid pouring out of the gap
where a cap should be and us staring
at the sudden change of circumstance.

We'd been moving so fast. Focused on the next place, the one after
that.

We'd used automatic cameras, yellow rolls of film.
We'd chosen our shots carefully, budgeting Tri-X squares for each
vision.
We note location and time in journals, like Weston and Lange,
sitting in the bar by the hostel, waiting for word on the car.
We imagine how each shot will look.
We anticipate what we think we saw: Contrast,
negative space, framing.

It's me who puts the yellow reels in a double-zip bag,
probably in the bar. Once the car is fixed
we debate whether to head back or keep going.
We drive to Cumberland Gap,
don't take photos: We're running out of film, tired from the road,
can't wait to get into a darkroom and discover what we've caught.

To pull the dark textures up from a white page.

Sometimes, what you don't see stays with you most.

The double-zip bag, when we open it, is nearly empty.
A receipt from the bar replaced our bone-dry red hills,
and the bar itself, the sandstone-drowned trees, the one moose.
The sunrises. The dogs.

A magic trick of sorts: the loss carves new spaces:
our journals, our notes on locations and times,
are white horizons we've fixed in our memories.

WINDOW

To the impure, all things are impure.   —Ed Weston

A razor-chafed pane in a desolate landscape.
A forgotten portrait. A windblown house,
its white caulk skeleton hardened
around each window seemingly
pure, bright squares,
but for their shadows, discarded pasts.

I read once that Weston worked for hours
to light a shell in such a way—now landscape, now vertebra
now voice—that it became a container for meaning.

So focused, Weston gave his house to the weather.
When windows burst, his son
scraped old photo plates with a razor,
leaving shadows of shadows on makeshift panes.

In that forgotten house, sunlight slipped
through shades: at midday, youngest daughter's portrait
bathed Weston's shell in a silk gown; by gloaming,
a landscape supported it, as if on a hillside.
Each pane keeping pace with the light,
adding its filter.

SELF PORTRAIT, WITH FEATHERED HEART

You can call me no name
not already inscribed, crimson,
deep in the curves of my feathered heart.
A ball of quilled words, grown sanguine,
clutched; a bird in my fist.

There's no vow I can make
from air or ink worth anything
until I write it down myself;
the barbs dig deep,
through what you say I am,

until the wet mess breaks
into a new language.
One you cannot call me in. One
that pounds against my fingers,
louder still.

DARKROOM

I.

In the darkroom's red safelight, my father teaches
me to twist knobs for focus,
to set timers, for exposure.

We set a negative to the enlarger's bit.
Pull paper from its sleeve,
        when we've got the image just right.
Then the timer starts; red disappears,
white light pinpoints features,
and a face comes clear,
darkness first, then highlights.
My face, all shadow, my hair like bone,
my mouth, my eyes, bone.
My soul on the page, a truth,
before the timer clicks, swapping white light
for red.
And I vanish.

A skeletal face reappears in the developing bath,
dark eyes properly shaded,
then a fixer buoys the contrasts, seals them in.

The darkroom's silence builds perfect, still images
no matter how much shouting happens
outside; here, shade and shadow appear

floating on expectation,
as I wait obediently, to witness what others see of me.

Stilled mouth, smiling eyes, ribbons of film
shine and shadow, a heavy distance draped
in the smell of chemicals
and, I guess, his wanting to teach me
something no one else could.

Red light: safe. White light: exposure.
        My face, blooming from white paper
if I get the timing right.
If not,
each bone sinks
into shadows pooling the edges,
and what defines me disappears.

II.

He won't remember the night of the fire.
He won't recall me, from my window, watching
him drag everything outside, the paper, the walls;

how everything went up, crisp ash-edged flame
twisting toward the pine tree by the driveway.
Negatives curl red and twist, lit by hand.

He keeps from the pyre a portait she disliked,
his proof, his right to burn everything else:
our history of silent road trips, innumerable fish on hooks,

two smiling girls, holding hands, their mother smiling,
everyone smiling, fire-curled.
Watching, I become complicit in his forgetting.

He's gone early the next morning, the driveway's cleaned,
the scorched branches of the pine tree the only witness
to the shadow-stained blacktop.

I pretend I dreamed it all—the fire,
his staccato shouts: *Everything burns; everyone lies*—
he'll forget, but I can't. She's begging for quiet, *Don't wake them.*

In the morning, she promises he'll be back.
"We're getting there. It will be all right."

Where is this *there* we're getting?
There is the fact of a cold, bare basement, a broken red light.

III.

A year later, another darkroom's built;
he hasn't burned anything in a while.
All the supplies, the bins, the lights
are new, and he rarely comes down.
I've become good at contrasts. Win a prize.

I spend a year away, then two.
He builds more pyres, of electronics, of kitchen utensils.
I'm living by the water when
my mother calls to tell me.

Her voice ripples: *All will be well.*

I watch a storm come from the east.
We're getting there, she says.
Boats drop sails, churn engines against the current.
I ask her where *there* is, and how far away.
A blink. A shutter closing over a lens.
She disappears and comes back.

Maybe, I think,
There is somewhere near
where my father flows and ebbs.

When I sign my next lease,
they send me the enlarger, the chemicals,
extra film.

IV.

I'd forgotten how paper floats white in a developing bath,
how darkness rushes up from the center, holds
for a moment within future shadows,
defines a remainder of white
to make a true portrait.

To the impure, all things are impure,
Ed Weston once said. I've watched from my window
knowing *there* wasn't getting closer
and we weren't heading toward it either
but I'd let her tell us anyway.

I pull out old albums, taped shut over empty pages.

Some photos I've burned myself

in a proper fireplace.

Others I wish I hadn't seen.

The prints of her, sliced at odd angles, pierced with holes.

In my small room by the water, I transform

with shutters and redlight,

I tell my mother I'm getting *there* too, though there isn't home.

I focus on his face in negative,

then let the paper glow white and empty for a moment,

before I lift it to the light.

COMET GARMENT

Take this, you'll do something with it.

Shimmering fabric, tucked here, gathered there,
and fit to itself with bright stitches;
you made a jacket of fiery movement.
Wore it only once.

Take this.

I find it in the back of your closet, after you go.
It hides among the old things, the rings and scarves,
the treasures, and your *Mad* magazines. I always wondered
where you hid those, when the ladies came by for bridge.

Now, in my own new city, I take your jacket, try it on.
I slip my arms in the too-long sleeves,
go out swinging at the darkness;
my fists sparkle.

You'll do something with it.

You'd sewn the jacket in New Orleans, wore it that once
but you weren't allowed to dance.
The buttons shine, it looks pretty on a thin frame—
wearing it takes some care, no one knows
we're standing still, even when we're not dancing.

Someone has had too much to drink
for us both. On the pier, my reflection tosses sparks at me.
A shooting star crosses the sky,
and you and I hang bright in the darkness.

Take this, you'll do something with it.

When you made it, you were new to town;
all the dancers were old, and they had you sit and watch
them: new gowns each night, all glitter and feathers, reveling
in exclusions. You never told anyone, before me.
You called it your ballgown jacket.

A lie is a flat surface gathered with truth, rolled up at the sleeves.
I can wear this all night, say it was my grandmother's ballgown
jacket,
though it's never been danced in.
Say this new city is so dull, but it's growing on me,
though no one's invited me anywhere.

Do something with it.
So tonight, I just do. I twirl and sparkle on the pier
with my reflections.

Later, the water and I will admit we'd both had too much
to drink; my reflection waves as I spin a hello
on the docks, light the night with sparks and I miss yous.

You made the jacket to spin like fire in a city rung with blues.
You made it before you knew guests could only watch.

Now I'm still trying it on,

trying to decide what to keep, how to dance,

which lie to put on in this new city of mine.

MY DAUGHTER TAKES UP SEWING

I will not tell her how fabric is a family blood sport,
thread and needle, guilt and gift, pin and cushion.

I won't say how often I failed to love enough
the patterns I was allowed, or removed wrong stitches late at night.

I don't mention the days before a dance spent waiting
for a dress to be perfected, to be finished in time.

I don't hint at how I wished for store-bought stability
without all the love sewn in.

Instead, I let her touch raw fabric in the store
sew without patterns
experiment with zippers and snaps
and put stripes and florals together,
lines mismatched at the seam.

I will not tell her how sharp my focus drew on a gather,
how each stitch had to be exact.

How my grandmother sewed until her eyes went
and my mother stitched late at night

and sometimes waited until the last minute to start a gown
so I'd value each hand-sewn edge, and know she loved me—
her eyes red, a Band-Aid on her finger—

at three o'clock, on the morning of a dance
when I wake to a perfect dress hung on my mirror
where there hadn't been one the night before.

Instead I tell my daughter she'll always have something to wear
to dance or to play in,
that she can always buy, or mend, or

make shapes from whole cloth
that drape her in glee,
spilling pins from the hem as she twirls.

SELF PORTRAIT, EDITED OUT OF PHOTOS

Self Portrait, Edited Out of Photos

Self Portrait as Letters I Have Not Sent

Self Portrait in X-rays

Self Portrait as a Series of Memes

Self Portrait in Fourteen Lines

Who Can Summarize Themselves in Fourteen Lines

Fourteen Lines Is for Other People

Self Portrait in Grief

Self Portrait with the Shoes I Bought To Feel Better

Self Portrait When the Shoes Do Not Fit

Self Portrait in the Dark

Self Portrait against a Night Sky

Self Portrait Not Floating, You're Floating

In a Night Sky, on a Blue Planet, So Very Far from Its Moon

III.

Rose:

DRAWING US DOWN
INTO THE WATER

THE HABIT OF THIS CREATURE IS TO DIVE FREQUENT
LY AND RISE AGAIN TO THE SURFACE WITH FISHES I
N ITS HANDS. WHEN SAILORS SEE IT PLAYING WITH
THE FISH, OR THROWING THEM TOWARDS THE SHIP
THEY FEAR THAT THEY ARE SO DOOMED TO LOSE S
EVERAL OF TH   SPECULUM REGALE
                                CIRCA 1250 AD

WHO AT F   RESOLVED TO
TAKE HER   NGING HE
R HOME   FED WITH
BREAD   MEATS A
NO WO   TO STEAL
AGAINT   THE SEA

SPECULU   MUNDI
JOHNS W   1635

THEY WER   PAINTED
A THOUGHT TO   A HUMAN A
PPEARANCE...   COLUMBUS 1492

THE ISLAND OF MI+   SOME FISHE
R MEN ENTRAPPED SEVEN,   OF WH
ICH SEVERAL JESUITS AND A   WERE
WITNESSES. THE PHYSICIA   WITH
A GREAT DEAL OF CAREA   AND
ASSERTS THAT THEIR INT   CTED THE   ER
ESEMBLED HUMAN BEING EXTERNAL ST   JOE
                 1560 CURIOUS MY

NIGHT WATCH

When we first moved to the rust city,
we kept watch for ways to be heroes,
found the abandoned, shipwrecked warehouses
filled with shadows and monsters. We sought those out.
Wove stories, as charms against danger.

We didn't see the slow terrors
as we searched for things to fight.

You didn't believe in charms, you said,
but monsters were okay. So we looked for monsters.

In the collapsing dark,
we climbed broken brick walls,
played a game of *What would you do if?*
We imagined fire and ash, zombies, floods;
hid quiet in our thoughts until
we were fearful enough
that a bag of trash became a body, face down,
a branch became a hand grabbing
from a torn grate.

But there was no body; the hand just a shadow
in flattened wharf grass. And the two of us,
practicing heroics,
caught in a searchlight, the police helicopter
swooping low over pilings and dark water, before
turning away.
The police, looking for a real body,
wanted nothing from us.
We disappeared into the shadows;
the red sugar factory sign rippled neon on the waves;

and wings knifed the air between us
and the water. I was afraid.
Helicopter light returned, haloed
a long sinuous neck and sharp beak.
A heron.
Always, before, seeing one had meant luck.
I pointed it out.

But you said herons don't come this far downtown,
Not with all the factories.
But here was one, still as glass, holding the night.
Its head, a blade, its body, a charred board, backlit black
by the gaining light, fishing the thick water as if we didn't matter.

The helicopter returned,
beating our ears with its wake
as it hovered over the empty lot.
The bird turned and stared in the metallic wind
and I felt the boundary of my skull within my skin
the cold of my bones, my eye rims.
Our shadows stretched long before us stalked the water.
Then the heron bent to fish again,
the helicopter flew away,
and I walked on with you,
my fingertip pulse pounding
though no monsters had been found.
It hadn't meant much to you, a heron
where there wasn't supposed to be one.

The city kept rebuilding itself.
The lot disappeared, the warehouse too.
I didn't see herons for a long time.
Later, the flood would come and the ash.
We talked to news cameras, held fundraisers.
We kept going, us and the city, rebuilding:
gleaming towers atop burnt piers, sunny days over moonless nights.
I remembered at times how a heron watched us holding hands
by search-churned water, playing at *what ifs* while we
imagined the night would show us something dangerous.

YOU ARE RESPONSIBLE FOR YOUR OWN WAKE

Out on the wooden dock beyond the city
two dinghies smack thick pilings thrown them
by the waves. A boat's speed cleaves the harbor,
and rocks them again. This time,
one thin hull defers to the dock's bulk, cracking
and its owner begins to shout *It's a slow zone*
Bastard come back here fucking . . .
but the shrill boat disappears, innocent.

In my hands, our collection of beach glass.
The swing of my arm casts wide
an arc of blue and green, sun-caught
glittering. Each fragmented bottle
transforms to stars, then
catches gravity and forges
swallowing sounds
before sinking deep.

Soon the water remembers
nothing of boat or beach glass.
I thought I'd lessen your effect
if I made a ritual; tossed these broken
containers in after you.

THE UNSEEN

When fog comes in,
fingertips pressing the windows,
it takes the distance first:
that mountain we always said we'd climb,
the tug in the harbor with its low horn,
the bridge's spun cables,
its arches.
The fog removes our familiar horizons
with its pale hands
and keeps coming.

How do you fight fog?

It seeps beneath doorways, wraps your throat,
slipping into mouth and ears,
stealing sound until the ship's horn becomes a sigh.
It comes for the houses, the doorknobs, the lights,
makes them soft, then holds them hidden.

But the tug knows to keep sounding,
the bridge plants its sturdy feet deep,
and you find your way out of doors
knowing the unseen mountain
is always there to climb.

WISH BOAT

Wishes float, you say,
casting a fistful of stale bread towards ducks
that have already eaten a lot of bread.
I almost miss the words between your pronouncements
on lunch (*gross*, again) and the substitute teacher
(*she laughs a lot, she taught us oregano*) as you sway,
four-year-old cheeks reddening in the wind.
Then you say it again. *Wishes float.*

Show me, I ask. You pull the paper from your backpack,
already creased. I can see where you wrote on it and erased,
before I picked you up, before we came out into the wind
to feed the now-forgotten ducks.
My own wishes sit tight at the back of my throat.
I want so many things today.
Four years ago, I wanted only one; made a silent promise
that if you lived, the universe could take me.
You live, and I have too so far, and so I get to watch you
kneel on the swaying dock and smooth the paper out.
Now all my wishes coil at my throat.
It's oregano, you say again, and I can't bear to tell you *origami*
I want the world to bend to your words instead

and I am still afraid to ask for anything else.
You press at corners, crease the folds,
make a small box: magic from a flat page.
You write your wish on a scrap of paper.
Your words float on the wind. *Now you,* you say.

THE DEEP

On open ocean,
a fistful of stars scattered
over waves.
Charts damp with spray,
numbered depths and distances
cite known risks, rocks
some other sailor found, once.

The sextant's out, measuring
a bow of sky,
the horizon's arc,
as night sounds the echoing deep.
And a small boat,
all creak and sway
climbs the moonlight.

SELF PORTRAIT AS A SELKIE

If I could peel my skin from its bones
and give it to you, I would—
if that would make you love me.
Not in the way you say you do,

not in the way you said I do.
In the way that would have you look at me
in wonder, the way I am
ocean and stars, wind and wildness.
See me for me:
   not by your side—your stalwart,
      your silent helpmeet—not your pretty bride.

If I could peel my skin back
and have you still love me then

I would do it over
and over again.

THE SEA NEVER SAYS IT LOVES YOU.

You could go to school with the sea.
You might pass it in the hall.
Maybe it asks you out. Maybe a movie
    or a dance—the waves curling about your ankles,
      people looking at you weird—
      but the water is warm and the salt spray tastes your lips
and you say yes.

You could marry the sea.
Might be it brings you pearls
or bright lights on the horizon blinking red and green and white,
a school of dolphins each day at two
to make you smile
but it never says anything
because it is the sea.

You could have the ocean's child.
A fish-pale, seaweed-haired shell
that splits you open and spills out
and you can watch everyone turn to catch it while you fall away.

You could walk by the sea in all seasons:
The season of umbrellas and noise.
The season of small dogs barking.
The season of strange machinery digging at the shoals.
The season of wind moving the water in new ways.

In those seasons, the walk will be comforting.
The sea is comforting in its strong silences.

But you cannot ask the sea to come to you and you cannot tell it
what you want,
for it is the sea, and it never really heard you
when it flooded the gates and overcame everything.

And you are bathed in salt spray, wishing
that you were water,
or that the sea would whisper from a shell the name of the first song
   you danced to.
Or say the name it gave you before it swallowed you up.

STORM TIDE

Most everyone on our street slept through
the night that water poured from the storm drains
and drowned the cars:
a slow apocalypse.
Chaos slid wet and dark, so quiet:
floated pets on cushions
sinking dining rooms river deep.

That night, we walked our streets like strangers
watching drains bubble, knocking doors
to wake those we could.
We went to bed at three a.m., convinced we'd seen
the worst out. The hurricane's turn
knotted the king tide
and drove the river forward,
sending the sirens into the hills.

In the morning,
a canoe passed below our window,
a bow-bound Odysseus wrapped in flannel,
with his six-pack
and a GoPro camera broadcasting live.

Emergency vans edged the neighborhood
handing out toothbrushes
to news crews, oracles
who asked us to stand closer to the waters' edge
for verisimilitude.

The other shore had it worse—
sirens beating the air, calling
at the deep bridges, the wrecked houses,
like ships now, facing the steadily rising water alone.

Water, like gods, doesn't stop when we ask it.
Slowly, through cracks, seeping,
rising from gutters and drains, back
where it had lived before we paved the city over it.
So quiet, so determined,
until there's an ocean in our living room,
until we are an island and there are birds
circling, taking photographs of the new landscape
and trading it to the mainland
for exposure. We are become scenery.

The night after the storm tide lifted doors
off the warehouses, rolled over the piers,
we woke to light rippling our ceiling
a seagull calling the bones at our window,
and sirens singing outside,
drawing us down into the deepening water.

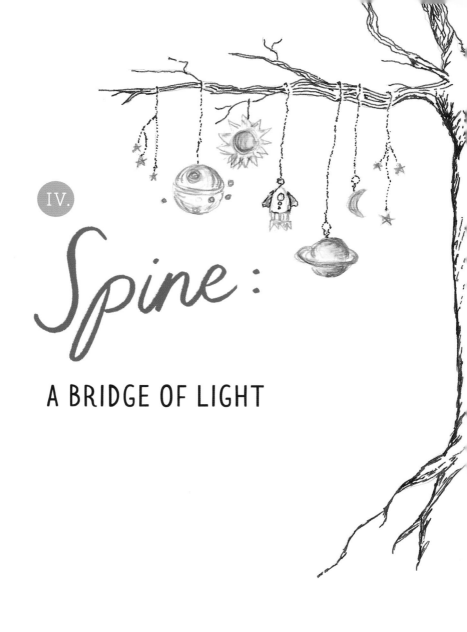

IV.

Spine:

A BRIDGE OF LIGHT

TERMS

This contract sets out
how I—a mouse, a hippocamp, a needle—
will occupy certain places, the walls
and air, the windows,
so that you will no longer be surprised:

In the restaurant, I will eat what I wish
    and no one will comment on whether it is too much or too
little.
In the restaurant, I will enjoy the taste of my food before I ask how
you like yours.
In the restaurant, I will taste food from my own fingers.
I will remember this moment, the spice of my skin and the salt too,
and it will not be taken from me and folded inside another moment
    where I feel ashamed.
Maybe the hippocamp's silver tail is a bit much
    for daytime,
but I like it, and I will be allowed to like things.

In the house, I will have my own opinions.
I will speak of my interests and you may,
    if you wish, pretend interest in my interests
until you are actively interested.
As one sometimes does. As I have done.
Sometimes this will pass for tenderness.
If you don't want to hear that your opinions are not mine also,
    and you feel this is cruel, my saying so,

Then I will be cruel.
Sometimes, in long relationships, tenderness can resemble cruelty.

In the doctor's office, I will describe my symptoms
to a stranger and they will listen and hear me
for those are two different actions.
In the doctor's office, where I've sat for a decade,
waiting for you to believe me,
all the instruments will turn to mice and run away,
while a monitor hawks the health dangers
    of too-muchness and too-littleism.
  There is nowhere to escape being told what we should be
      for other people.
        My teeth will shred the broadcast, cable and screen.
In the doctor's office, the lights will dim
and someone will write "I believe you" on a chart
and I will finally relax.

In this contract, I will speak and you will hear me,
even if I whisper.
These are my terms for continuing.
I will pass through rooms and streets like a mouse
or a needle or a water horse
if I choose.
I will wear a skirt of dust or a crown of teeth
or seventeen rings on ten fingers
or all of the above.
If you have questions you can ask but I do not have to answer.
You will see me.
You will be as present for me as I am for you.

In the museum, I will look at a painting.

The frame of the painting won't match the swirl of pigment it traps.

I will see a flick of silver tail, and the artist—

    her shadow will creep around the edges of the frame, prying it loose—

    I might follow the artist into the painting. I might not.

In the museum, I will look at this painting, and that sculpture.

I will do so without your hands on mine.

I will let the air frame me.

I will like the art that I like, and I will not care if you don't.

In the bathroom, I will shut the door and you will not open it.

In the bathroom, I'll look at myself in a mirror

    and think that maybe I am beautiful, still, although you rarely say it.

In the bathroom, I'll paint my palms silver and press them to the mirror

until I disappear.

  I am allowed to disappear.

Sometimes people disappear.

Sometimes when they do, like a needle, like a silver tail,

they will pull all their world through the mirror with them.

Sometimes you won't notice. Sometimes

it will make you angry and you will yell

because the hippocamp really was a bit much, and the mouse too.

You want a prop, or a mirror.

You want what doesn't change shape very fast,

    something easily framed.

Above all else, you want to be seen as expert on the subject of me.

In that desire, you are reading this contract as a way to become expert.

And I am laying out my terms for never that.

LELLOW

The word bubbles up,
punctuating recognition:
the color
your favorite
your joy
is *lellow*.
You laugh and I kiss your fat cheeks
and we hold the color you now know
the word beautiful on your lips
not yet fully formed.
I know you will find the why and the how of it
and you will trade these sounds
for other ones.
But I gather this word up like spring's first bloom
and press it close.

THEFT

—for Mia—

The morning the officials
Stole all the words,
We bit into apples sliced thin
And drank coffee, not noticing
That the table had disappeared,
    The window,
Even as we talked and chewed and laughed.

Friends wrote columns of blank space
Demanding a return
Of sense and empathy
And officials heard the
    And saw the

Then they returned our words
In sacks. Gave them back
To us upside down.
So we sit at the thin
And we sip at a table
And we bite into windows

The brittle glass stinging our tongues.
We refuse to stop chewing.

TELL IT SLANT

My photographs begin to skew again.
My perspective, my lens
tilts to the left, the right, a seasick horizon,
each river or sea in each background
pooling damp in your lap,
wet on the floor.
Each frame drained of substance,
each foreground hung to dry.

The black and white of me, tilted.
Stacks of film, books of images, spines
like rivers turning their gyres, each
vertebra marking a point of departure
from normal. Angles
match edges, form curves. My images,
my skeleton, my frame is complex geometry
drawing pale numbers in the black.

To reach one point from another in space
you cannot fly straight.
There's no crow to guide you
only curves in the dark, calculations
and measurements, a few moments of hope.
We used to trace our paths by shoreline, by clock tick
by knotted rope, feeling our way,
then praying we'd come close
but not too close.

Now we take soundings with our phones,
know our exact geometry, where the point
that is us meets the curve of the world, our latitude
and longitude, to as many degrees as necessary.

We take photographs, snap them up by the handful,
pile pixels in storage somewhere out there—
each tiny square tagged with its own data: time and place,
speed, distance from and to. We know the coordinates
of each body we create, all our numbers.
We are sure of them, thinking these will help us find
ourselves if we are ever lost.

They begin to skew when no one's looking.
Spines and rivers, pictures and points.
    All these coordinates
want to flow like water
want to run from the frame
and be unfindable again, extraordinary
uncountable, painful even,
resistant to our devices,
our braces and boxes,
our maps and arcs, our words
not points and pixels laid
but the river of light that becomes them.

BRIDGE, BRANCH

Entering the morning
climbing through air:
rose light on shadowed branches
and a distant hawk wings
up, up.
My eyes follow, my arms
want to be weightless
to lift without hurt.
This is so hard to convey
from one body to the next.
Describing beauty
extends a bridge, a connection.
Writing pain threads dark cracks
through rose skies:
the hawk hunts the air,
carves with its passage
deep gaps
in the bare distances.

ORRERY

After the Rittenhouse Orrery at Princeton, 1771

A universe on a spindle,
clockwork stars,
hand-turned brass and glass orbit
as gears twirl sun, moon, ring, and shadow
to a different kind of time.

Even the word does what it says
each 'r' spun around the big 'O'
then a ripple repeating until the 'y'
whips a comet's tail, a wonder
of engineering, a vivid mimic.

Spool the universe forward or back
a thousand years, more.
See where planets were and will be
according to their maker,
how each slides past others, elliptical;
a family tied at the base,
turning now close, now away.

Generations move past old collisions,
rotate around missing moons
and forgotten tugs of gravity
as if the oracle of planets steered us wrong
when we stopped looking for each other

across the sun's broad sphere
and focused on the predictable instead.

Above the gears, the sky hides
a deeper spin. All our efforts to understand
the distances between one planet and the next
one person and the next
are signals passed back and forth, pulses of light
half understood as we try to shape meaning
from symbols.

MOVING ON

The world wakes up, makes coffee sounds
while you're still mourning someone not dead

having buried their shadow around midnight,
traveled back home through memory's decades,

and arrived silent at your own street, your steps,
your door, your clean kitchen.

You: cobweb-covered, clumps of dark dreams weighing
your boots, a shovel cold on your shoulder.

The sun outlines orange the winter trees;
white mugs clink against white tile.

SELF PORTRAIT, AS LUGGAGE

How much can you carry, leather-bound
your heart tight packed, folded beneath sweaters.
The bag's seams wear-worn and greasy,
its sides slouched, waiting, near the dark tunnel.

How many memories should you haul,
what can you press inside and zip shut?
What drags against your rush and hurry
wanting to slow you down.

What has been crushed and how often,
what will soon burst at the seams;
the ripe pulp of dirty socks spills
just as the tunnel fades train bright.

This bag is not for round trips or delays.
It is determined to go only one way.

NOTES ON REENTRY

A streak of light against sky
    an object moving faster
    than space around it can bear.
    A stone has grazed the roof of the world
    and the space beyond it
    and wishes to return, bearing
    all it knows now
    that it didn't know before.

The roof of the world
    closes in.
    There's nothing it needs to know.
    The sky is blue, the clouds are white.
    A charred star
    that once explored
    once moved fast
    now rests stilled and small
    in the cage of the earth.

SELF PORTRAIT AS EVENT HORIZON

The gravity of any situation: fear's depths,
the dark's best monster—
a closet of space, eating stars.
My heart beats sometimes so full
      with every failing
      it collapses,
drags everything through physics' needle
to a pain-dense point, with no exit.

Post-collapse: redshift beyond gravity.
The stubborn star's pulse still signaling.
One beat and then the next; if I survived,
what else is out here in the velvet deep?

A light winks, curious, beyond the void,
and my heart inevitably follows.

POSTSCRIPT: INK NOTES

1 Hi, Fran! You're mostly known as a writer of prose fiction, but *Clock Star Rose Spine* is an illustrated collection of poetry. Can you tell us a little bit about your background in poetry and visual art?

One of the elements I like most about poetry is how it weaves connections. Between white space and letterforms on the page. Between image and sound. Between one instance of a word and the next. Each helps the poem build even more connections in the reader's mind.

When I studied poetry as an undergraduate at University of Virginia, my teachers—including Rita Dove and Charles Wright—helped me look at the way words built those connections in completely new ways. I kept doing that at the Warren Wilson MFA for Writers near Black Mountain, NC, studying with Heather McHugh, Eleanor Wilner, Marianne Boruch, Larry Levis, and others (including Tony Hoagaland, Agha Shahid Ali, and Ellen Bryant Voigt)—all of whom encouraged me to look and read, and also to live while writing, because neither poetry nor connections happen in a vacuum. I finished a manuscript at Warren Wilson, before other studies (an MA in information architecture and interaction design) and work (game design, graphic design, teaching) drew me away from poetry for a long time. Still, I maintained connections: with the visual artwork I'd been doing since high school; with language.

When I began to write more fiction—starting with flash (which is very much like poetry in that it has very little space to form connections, so each word must do three times the work) and eventually working my way up to novels—I knew all the way that there were poems waiting for me. My fiction has songs and poems, repetition and connection woven through it. I was reading poetry too, trying to find that place where literary writing and speculative writing dovetailed. I found it in the poetry of Tracy K. Smith, Pablo Neruda, Wisława Szymborska, and Rachelle Cruz. I found it in music, in that perfectly metered first line of a novel that grabs you and won't let you go. But it wasn't until 2016 that I started really writing my own poems again, with a new sense for language and image, sound and word—gained from experience. And these poems took a very different shape from the earlier work I'd been doing.

When the images started to join in, especially as I wrote and drew in my journals, I could see connections happening between and among each work—and across the work too. From drawing to poem and back. That's when *Clock Star Rose Spine* really started to take shape.

2   What pens and inks did you use in this book?

I used two Sailor Procolors and two TWSBI Ecos. The Procolor Shikisai Stardust (fine nib) is loaded with Sailor Black ink. The Procolor Shikisai Blue (fine nib) is loaded with OS Nitrogen. The TWSBI Ecos are both extra-fine nibs and hold Pilot Iroshizuku Ina-Ho ink and Diamine Aurora Borealis, respectively. I also use a $4 waterbrush.

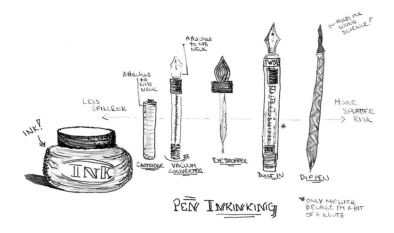

INK!

LESS SPILL RISK ←

→ MORE SPLATTER RISK

Attaches to NIB NECK

Attaches to NIB NECK

← HOLDS INK USING SCIENCE?

INK

CARTRIDGE   VACUUM CONVERTER

EYEDROPPER

BUILT IN

DIP PEN

PEN INKINKING

*ONLY MESSIER BECAUSE I'M A BIT OF A KLUTZ

③ How does hand drafting influence your writing process?

It's messier, but when I hand-draft, I can also see where I've been. Writing on a computer means that elision is easy, as is the illusion of instant perfection. Hand drafting means we are always reminded that revision is necessary, and that crossing things out creates its own resonances on the page.

④ Writing with fountain pens is a lot messier and more involved than writing with regular pens, especially if you're using bottled ink and have to refill a converter. What draws you to it?

It's thoughtful. There's a process to it. And a constancy—refilling pens reminds me to refill my brain with others' words too.

5 How old were you when you first discovered fountain pens? Did teenage Fran have an ink collection, or did that happen later?

Teen Fran did NOT have an ink collection, other than the drawing pens I used for my artwork! This is fairly new—early 2010 to 2011, when a programming friend and a writing friend both recommended TWSBI pens around the same time. The ink obsessions inevitably followed.

6 Say you're talking to someone who's never written with a fountain pen before. What parts does it have? How do they work?

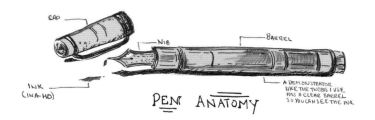

CAP
NIB
BARREL
INK
(IN A-HD)
A DEMONSTRATOR LIKE THE TWSBIS I USE HAS A CLEAR BARREL SO YOU CAN SEE THE INK
PEN ANATOMY

7 Sounds like an expensive hobby. Don't fountain pens cost hundreds of dollars?

Some pens are collectors' items (i.e., trophy pens) and those do cost a LOT. Others are more practical. I love the TWSBI lines because they hold a lot of ink and are light and cost-efficient ($30-70) while being sturdy and long-lasting. And when they do stop being long-lasting, you can keep the parts and franken-pen new ones together. Jin-hao pens and Lamys are also worth considering. And (when I'm at home) I have a glass dip pen that cost $25, which is both fun to write with and beautiful, without needing to load a lot of ink.

(7A) How much does a newbie have to spend to get started? What's a good "starter set"?

Try a few pens out—either by going to a pen meetup or talking to a friend—and you'll discover what size pen, weight, and nibs you like to write with. You can get a Jin-hao or a Lamy for under $20. And you can come by an ink sampler to see what kinds of inks you like from stores like Gouletpens.com for $10. The best starter set is a pen you'll use, and ink you like.

(8) What is your favorite ink color?

Blues—all of them. And black.

. . . just like my wardrobe. Huh. Hadn't thought about that.

Favorites currently are: OS Nitrogen, Hisoku (a pale blue that washes beautifully), Diamine Aurora Borealis, and Colorverse Eagle.

NOTES

"Theft" was written for my friend after her mother was put on trial in the Philippines by President Rodrigo Duterte.

"Tell It Slant" takes its title from Emily Dickinson's "tell all the truth, but tell it slant."

"Orrery" is inspired by the Rittenhouse Orrery at Princeton.

The Lafayette Hotel in "Breakfast Poolside at the Lafayette" was opened in 1946 by developer Larry Imig as a retreat for Hollywood stars.

"Looking Back: Exhibition in Red" was inspired by the Louise Bourgeois Retrospective at MoMA, 2017–18.

The epigram in "Window" comes from photographer Ed Weston's notes on the photograph "Pepper No. 30". The photographer used old photographic plates to patch windows.

"You Are Two Point Three Meters from Your Destination" is a retelling of Orpheus and Eurydice via GPS directions. All distances but the descent into Hades were calculated using historical references, consultation with classicists, and Google Maps. While historical measurements would have been in steles, GPS directions are not.

"You Are Responsible for Your Own Wake" takes its title from a cautionary sign in Baltimore's Inner Harbor.

While there are many floods it could describe, the poem "Storm Tide" originated during Hurricane Isabel, 2003.

PUBLICATION HISTORY

"Theft" originally appeared in *Who Will Speak for America* (Temple University Press, 2018).

"You Are Two Point Three Meters from Your Destination" originally appeared in *Uncanny Magazine* (2016).

"The Sea Never Says It Loves You" originally appeared in *Uncanny Magazine* (2018) and was a 2018 Rhysling Award finalist.

"The Unseen" originally appeared in *Fireside Magazine* (2019) and was a 2019 Rhysling Award finalist.

"Night Watch" appeared in a different form in *Poetry Baltimore* (Word House Press, 1997).

ACKNOWLEDGMENTS

To my teachers, both in and out of the classroom: Rita Dove, Debra Nystrom, Charles Wright, Ellen Bryant Voight, Heather McHugh, Larry Levis, Joan Aleshire, Marianne Boruch, Tom Lux, Chip Delany.

To wonderful fellow travelers in verse—poets, teachers, dreamers, and editors alike—especially Julia Rios, Laura Gray Street, Peg Alford Pursell, CSE Cooney, Stephanie Feldman, Mimi Mondal, Michi Trota, Brandon O'Brien, Amal El-Mohtar, Theodora Goss, Deborah Artman, Ali Trotta, Kat Howard, Sam Miller, and Carlos Hernandez.

To the places and people that have published, supported, cheered, and guided me while I worked on this collection, including: Warren Wilson MFA for Writers, the University of Virginia, Kickstarter Creators in Residence, Western Colorado University

Graduate Program in Creative Writing, *Uncanny Magazine*, *Fireside Magazine*, *Poetry Baltimore*, Temple University Press, and, very importantly, all the members of my Patreon who made the last stretch possible.

To everyone at Lanternfish Press—especially Christine, Feliza, and Amanda—who has hauled this gorgeous book out of the sea with me—I cannot thank you enough. It's more than I ever dreamed possible.

And most of all, to my family, far and wide, especially Tom and Iris, Sue and Chris.

ABOUT THE AUTHOR

FRAN WILDE is the double Nebula-award-winning author of seven novels for children and adults, as well as numerous short stories, reviews, and essays that cross literary and genre boundaries. Trained as an artist, jeweler, programmer, and poet, Fran received her MFA in poetry from Warren Wilson College and an MA in interaction design from the University of Baltimore. She is the genre fiction concentration director at Western Colorado University. This is her first collection of poetry and illustration.